The View from My Chair

IN CHINA

THIS IS A JOURNAL I KEPT ON A TWO WEEK STUDY ABROAD SESSION SPONSORED BY TROY UNIVERSITY'S CONFUCIUS INSTITUTE

BENJAMIN MAXWELL

June 24/25, 2011 – Day 1

The day began about 5:00 am in Atlanta. My friends Melanie, Karli, Steven and myself woke up early and got ready to battle the Thursday morning city traffic. After what seemed liked hours of being hoarded through line after line in the airport we were finally on our way to Chicago's O'Hare airport.

After arriving in Chicago we quickly embraced our nine hour lay-over by catching the "Blue Line" tram and headed towards downtown Chicago. After walking around for about an hour and taking in the large city while looking for looking for a signature Chicago place to eat lunch we finally found ourselves at a small pizza place called Lou Malnatis for lunch. We indulged in the local authentic deep-dished pizza. We spent the next few hours wandering around the city seeing as much as we could, including the Sears Tower and Wrigley Field. Finally it was back to the airport for our flight to Beijing!

We left Chicago about 9:00 pm on a massive Boeing 777. The flight took us over Canada, over the top of Alaska, across the international dateline and down through Russia to Beijing. The flight lasted almost 13 hours, which I miraculously was able to embrace with some sleep.

We arrived in Beijing around 11:00 pm on June 24 (Friday night). Stepping off the plane in the Beijing airport it was impossible not to be overwhelmed by the size of the airport - this is in comparison to both the Atlanta and Chicago airports. It might have been the size of the structure or the time of night but it was not very crowded. That is until we found ourselves back in more lines and herded back onto trams.

My first impression of the Chinese people was that everyone seemed focused on their own business and unconcerned about those around them. Families stick close and move together; not many children were running around unattended. They appeared as a well disciplined people.

When I finally stepped outside I took in my first breath of Beijing air. I was a little surprised when I was not hit by any distinct smell or taste, although it was no surprise to find that there was no refreshing feeling from the air. It is no secret that the air quality here in China is far from the best and one is quickly reminded of that with each breath.

Leaving the airport we hoped on one of many buses waiting outside. All cars, trucks, and buses in China appeared to have a type of uniformity in size and color. The road directly leaving the airport had no median lines, which one would think would cause chaos but besides an inconvenient traffic jam at a toll booth everything moved efficiently.

The city had a feel of uniformity as well, but one thing that stood out was the effort the city took in its beautification. Along the major highway and every exit ramp were large carefully pruned bushes. The city was clean and orderly, although it is almost mid night.

At about one in the morning we finally arrived at our hotel which turned out to be a Best Western. It was unlike the Best Western's in America. This hotel had a five star feel with its elaborate floor plan and chauffeurs outside. Each room in the hotel had internet, although sites like Facebook, Twitter, and YouTube were all blocked.

June 25 – Day 2

Our first day in China began with a large breakfast at the hotel. The breakfast spread was much larger than the typical hotel breakfast back home. It consisted of a variety of interesting Chinese dishes. I tried everything. One of my favorite items was actually the yogurt cups. They looked like normal yogurt cups but it is sipped through a straw and it has a salted butter taste instead of the sweet sugar taste of the typical yogurt cups at home.

After breakfast I went to the front desk of the hotel to exchange my U.S. currency into Yuan. For every $100 I received 640 Yuan (元 or ¥). Although there was one twenty dollar bill the cashier would not exchange because she claimed it was too worn.

Our first excursion of the trip - and probably the most anticipated - was at the Great Wall of China. It took about an hour by bus to get there from our hotel. On the way we were able to see the vastness of the city of Beijing.

The traffic was congested all through the city. Traffic here is much tighter and was a chaotic display of drivers cutting one another off and passing each other by mere inches. Whenever a driver was disgruntled they announced it with a quick honk of their horn. This causes a constant sound of honking - it really becomes aggravating after a while. There is an unofficial rule among drivers that the smaller vehicle must yield to the bigger one - which seems like a basic natural law.

On the way to the Great Wall we left the city and entered into an enormous landscape of steep mountain ranges. The mountains were more rocky and serrated than the mountains I am used to back in north Alabama. At the bottom of the mountains were small villages scattered about. There were people working on their homes on what appeared as a typical Saturday morning. Throughout the mountains were sections of the Great Wall that appeared sporadically out of nowhere, ran up the mountains and disappeared on the other side. The road we were on wrapped around the rugged landscape and through tunnels that were dug through the mountains.

When we arrived at the section of the Great Wall where we would spend the morning we encountered thousands of people from all over the world as well as many locals. After satisfying many of our groups "Kodak moments" we began our climb up the wall. It is said that anyone who climbs to the top of the wall is thought of as a hero. I accepted that challenge and headed to the top with Steven. In some areas the wall was sloped which seemed easier to scale than the areas that had steps. To get to the top the biggest challenge was battling the hoards of people. The wall jumped up and down over the rough terrain. Just when the wall appeared to disappear it popped up again on an adjacent hill. The beautiful day fed the awesome scenery. After making it to the top we promptly had to descend back to the bottom to meet with our group at a small coffee shop just outside the wall.

At the wall our group got one of the biggest culture shocks, when we encountered for the first time the Chinese bathroom. The toilets in China are literally in the ground and to use it one must squat over it instead of comfortably sit down like back home.

Leaving the Great Wall we headed back into the city for lunch. The place we went to was on the second floor of a pottery factory. We watched as many young to middle age women designed many different intricate designs on varied sizes of pots and vases. After receiving paint the pottery is polished by men with different types of stones.

Lunch consisted of familiar entrees of rice, noodles, sesame chicken, and vegetables. When we finished eating we were allowed back downstairs to shop from the store which was right outside the factory.

We then headed back through the city to the "Ming Tomb" – the tomb of Chang Ling; one of the more well-known tombs in Beijing. Throughout the city there is a network of tombs. At the entrance of the network of tombs was a large marble gate. Back in ancient times if a ruler wanted to visit the tombs he would ride his horse to this gate, dismount his horse at the gate and walk the rest of the way to the tomb he would visit. This was mandated on a stone next to the gate. If the emperor were to visit Chang Ling's tomb he would have to enter through another gate and into a court yard. In the court yard was a large palace dedicated to Emperor Chang. Behind the palace was another gate which one could only go through when leaving. When entering past the gate one must pass around the right side. While passing through this gate on the way out men must cross the threshold starting with their left foot and the women with their right foot. To step on a threshold of a door or gate anywhere in China was very disrespectful and was like standing on the shoulders of the host of the home. Behind this gate was another temple on top of a wall which circled a small hill. This hill is where the emperor is buried, although it is unknown the exact location of the actual body of the Emperor in the hill.

After visiting the tomb it was on to a Jade factory. Jade is a precious stone that is a signature emblem of China. Jade is the second hardest stone in the world – next to the diamond. Jade carving is a family trade. To be a jade carver one must be born into or marry into the family. Two thirds of the countries jade carvers worked in this particular factory. Jade has four main colors: green, purple, yellow, and white. The stone is beautiful and is carved into just about anything. My particular favorite carving of the stone is called the "Happy Family Ball." It is a round shape that is carved in many sizes with a different number of layers inside the shape.

Each layer moves around freely inside the other layer.

Leaving the Jade factory we headed to one of Beijing's Olympic parks for dinner. The parks were created in 2008 when China hosted the Olympics. Dinner was almost an exact replica of lunch, except for the fish that was served in its entirety – head included. This was a little disconcerting for some members of our group. Hearing that the head of any animal in many cultures is the ultimate delicacy I gave it a shot. It was not as bad as it appeared, except for the sweet and sour sauce that added an odd sweet taste to a naturally salted taste.

We returned to the hotel after dinner but before returning to our rooms a few of us walked down the crowded street to the local grocery store which was actually called "Wu Mart." It was very similar to the grocery stores back home except that it was in a basement. There were escalators at the main entrance that took us down into the store. The meat department had a larger selection of what would be unusual choices back home. They had every part of every kind of animal out on display for selection. The air conditioner – much like every other place in Beijing – was not running to the same capacity that I'm used to. This gave a humid un-refreshing feel that I eventually forced myself to adjust to.

The whole group at the Great Wall

June 26 – Day 3

We started our day off with quick trips to Qinghua University and Beijing University. Both universities were beautiful with old detailed buildings. Although the college grounds lacked the same grounds keeping standards than the American university counter parts. The grass around the buildings in many areas was almost thigh high.

Both universities had families walking around with students dressed in their graduation gowns. Being Sunday morning it reminded me of graduations back home with all of the families walking around campus posing for pictures in every corner of the university with their children.

After visiting the universities we traveled to the Ruined City. The Ruined City is what is left of one of the giant summer palaces of the emperor that was destroyed by western powers in the nineteenth century. The city was vast and elaborate. Much of it had not even been touched since being reduced to ruble. One section of the city was a maze structured by deep gray stone that stood about five feet high. At the center of the labyrinth was a small white marble gazebo looking structure.

At the ruined city we found a new building that had been added more recently. Inside the building was a giant scaled down model of what the city looked like in its heyday. Outside the building we found black swans in one of the ponds.

After the Ruined City it was on to lunch. It was much like the day before. The restaurant was on the second floor of a building. The first floor was a pearl shop. After we ate we went downstairs for a pearl harvesting demonstration.

Next it was on to Fragrant Hill. Steven and I accompanied by one of the Troy professor's with us, Pete, were the only ones of our group to actually climb to the top of the hill. It took us a little over an hour to reach the top. During the climb we were motivated by spectacular views overlooking the city of Beijing as well as peaceful trails that winded through the hill. We passed many people on the way up. I took this as an opportunity to practice my mandarin. Everyone we passed who I said "Nin Hao" to smiled with excitement that I was speaking their language.

A few replied with phrases that I was unfamiliar with, but I tried to hide my lack of knowledge with phrases like:

It's too hot! – (Tài zshula) - 太热

At the top of the hill was a wide panoramic view of the city. The city stretched as far as the eye could see in all directions – it was vaster than any other city I have ever seen. I found it interesting to see two nuclear power plants off to the left of the hill considering I have only seen one nuclear plant back home.

At the top of the hill was a cable car that carried people from the top of the hill to the bottom. Unfortunately for us the cable car was closed for the day and we were running short on time to meet the group back at the bottom. That is when we bumped into a local who did not speak English but was trying to gesture that he had another way down the hill. After finding another local who spoke a little English we found out that he was trying to tell us he had a van that could carry us to the bottom.

To get to the van we had to climb up a wooden ladder over a stone wall and down another wooden ladder. This process began to make Pete, Steven, and I wonder about what we were getting into, but we needed to get to the bottom quickly so we proceeded. Once in the van and after an intense process of price haggling with the man we headed down the hill. The road was concrete and clanged tightly to the back side of the hill on one side of the road and on the other side was a steep drop with no railing. It was a precipitous and terrifying ride at high speeds with sudden jerks of the brakes as we hooked around tight turns.

Fortunately we finally made it to the bottom unscathed; however it was on the other side of the hill. We then had to walk around the hill to the opposite gate on the south side of the hill. We found ourselves walking through allies of small villages that rested against the base of the hill. Steven, Pete, and I finally found ourselves back to the group having conquered Fragrant Hill.

Steven, Pete and me after conquering Fragrant Hill

June 27 – Day 4

Today began at the Confucius institute. The building was simple and a squared design on the outside but inside had a modern state of the art feel. There was information stations set up to teach visitors about all aspects of Chinese culture including language, music, clothing, food, and the diversity of the city. My favorite station was a giant bowl in the middle of the floor. It had an interactive screen inside that displayed the evolution of the Chinese written language.

I also learned how to sign my name in Chinese:

Benjamin - 本杰明 (Běnjiémíng)

Next it was onto our next biggest culture shock, the Buddhist temple. The temple was laid out much like the tombs from the day before. It was a series of buildings arranged one after another where one had to pass through one temple to get to the next temple. In each building were different Buddha statues with each one serving a different purpose. For example, there was the "Happy Buddha" for fortune and good luck as well as the Buddha's for past, present, and future.

Outside each palace were altars for burning incense. The smell from the incense mixed with the smell from the sewer which ran underneath the temple to create an overwhelming odor that stole my attention away from fully taking in the entire temple. In the last temple was a large three to four story Buddha statue. This statue was to represent Buddha itself. We were strongly discouraged from taking pictures inside the actual temples; this was a custom we ran into all over Beijing in most of the spiritual themed buildings.

Next was lunch. Again it was just like the meals we had eaten for the previous two days; however the building resembled more of a restaurant than the previous places we had eaten at. Much like the previous restaurants we sat at round tables and all the food was placed on a round turn table in the center of the table.

One thing I have had to adjust to is that back home I am used to waiting for everyone at the table to receive their food before eating but here as soon as the food hits the table everyone begins digging in. The Chinese people educate at the dinner table is much different than back home as well. Here the food is brought up close to the face and then shoveled into the mouth.

The more I eat the food here the more the smell of the city makes sense. The smell of the food is like a backbone for all of the smells in the city. Whether it is from smell of the public bathrooms or the smell of the people themselves on the street, all the smells are variations of the smell of the food.

After lunch it was on to the Imperial University and Confucius temple. This temple was dedicated to one of the most well known thinkers in the world. We discovered that the wisdom of Confucius was never fully respected until after death, now he may be one of the most quoted philosophers in the entire world. One of my favorite parts of the temple was a statue of Confucius posed to look like he was teaching. It forces one to imagine what it must have been like to hear from this one man who is so widely touted as being so wise.

Next it was on to a Kung Fu show – which was impressive display of kung fu skills with a small plot mixed in. However, before the Kung Fu show we killed some time at the Pearl Market. The market was a five story building full of enthusiastic vendors whose only goal is: SELL! SELL! SELL! Here I discovered a natural skill that I never knew I had: haggling.

In many cases I negotiated prices of ¥180 and ¥190 down to ¥20 and ¥40. I ticked off a few vendors with steep undercutting of their initial price but all you can do is just ignore most vendors. Many of them seem to have a short memory of customers anyway. Some vendors were more emphatic than others and would chase customers down and pull them towards their booth. One lady pulled me aside and physically would not let me go until I finally pulled away from her and quickly walked away.

The market was almost overwhelming on initial impression. However, with its many stories of hundreds of vendors, one begins to realize all of the merchandise is essentially the same. It is just about finding the right vendor worth dealing with.

Key phrases in the Pearl Market:

Too much! - **太多** (Tài duō)

No thank you - **不**, 谢谢 (Bù, xièxiè)

Despite aggravating many of the vendors most of them complimented me on my haggling skills. One in particular was on the third floor of the market, her name was Lulu. After an intense negotiation she posed for a picture with me. As we stood there in the middle of the market tossing jokes and compliments at one another I noticed all of the other vendors began to stop and watch Lulu and me. Their shy expressions slowly turned to comfortable happy smiles. I felt like I made an actual friend in Beijing.

My original impression of the cleanliness of the city of Beijing quickly subsided. There seems to be no laws or concerns for littering. In some areas of the city the garbage is pushed into piles where it looks like it is then left and forgotten. The only counter for this problem is some of the older folks collect plastic bottles to recycle for money. Many of them have no problem of taking the bottles right out of my hand and backpack. In one case one lady pointed at the water bottle in my backpack as if she was asking for it, in which case I quickly chugged the rest of the water and handed it over to her.

People here also have no problem relieving themselves in the streets. Just today in the Buddhist temple I saw a little boy relieving himself into one of the drainage vents in the middle of the temple.

People here are actually very friendly; that is if you initiate the greeting. People often do not speak unless spoken to and come across as shy. It is easy to see that free thinking is not as highly encouraged here.

After three days of nothing but honking from the traffic, which I can still hear from the hotel room, I find myself beginning to forget about it. Also I have noticed that as crazy as the traffic is, I have not seen any wrecks. Maybe chaos works.

Being Monday – our first weekday in Beijing – the smog appears to be growing thicker.

Statue of Confucius

June 28 – Day 5

The day started with a trip to Tiananmen Square. It was exactly as its name describes – a big open square. The square is the center piece of surrounding buildings like the national museum, Chairman Mao's mausoleum and the Forbidden City. In the center of the square was a large image of a hammer and sickle with 1921-2011 engraved under it.

At the front of the square rests the entrance of the Forbidden City. At the entrance is a large mural of Mao. There were a lot of people there but it was not as crowded to where it was hard to move around. After posing for many pictures on the square, we crossed the street through an underground tunnel to the other side to the Forbidden City.

The Forbidden City's architecture and layout was much like the tombs and temples we had visited earlier except it was much larger. To see every inch of the city would take days. It consisted of palace after palace, each one surrounded by a stone laid courtyard. There were no trees or flowers in the courtyards to allow the city to appear bigger thus making the emperor feel mightier.

Lunch, again was another restaurant with the familiar spread of the previous days, followed by shopping at a little street of antique shops. Then it was on to the silk factory.

At each restaurant we were given tea to drink. The tea does not have much flavor at all and is as refreshing as drinking boiled water. It is meant to be revitalizing. Along with the tea we are given one glass of our choice of Coke, Sprite, or beer – refills typically cost extra, but the tea is endless.

The power grid of the city seems stretched a little further than back home. It is HOT! ...EVERYWHERE! We have a small fridge in our hotel room but it never gets cold. There is a slot by the door of our room where we place the room key while we are in the room. By placing the card in the slot allows for the power to run in the room, but when we take our key out when we leave kills the power; this includes the air conditioner. When we return to our rooms it is hot and we have to crank up the air conditioner all over again. The air conditioner however is futile to countering against the heat.

My roommate, Steven and I tried to counter this one day by one of us leaving behind our key card in the slot when we departed. However we returned to find that the card had been removed and left on the desk in the hotel room.

Every place we have been to that does have air conditioner seems weak compared to the air conditioner back home. Finding a cold drink is also a battle; however I'm starting to adapt to the heat, sweating everywhere I go, and drinking room temperature beverages.

Steven and myself outside the entrance to the Forbidden City

June 29 – Day 6

It is Wednesday morning here in Beijing and the smog is stronger than ever. Last night a few of us got a chance to get out of the hotel and experience a little of the Beijing night life.

Steven and I took a cab through the city with Pete to meet with a few other students who also decided to break the tourist monotony. They were accompanied with a few locals as well. The cab was a much welcomed break from the cramped tour bus. The notorious Beijing traffic is much worse outside the large frame of our bus. I would really hate to see what these people spend on the maintenance of their brakes from all the instant stops from constantly being cut off.

Walking down the streets, I started getting the feeling that I was finally experiencing the TRUE Beijing culture away from the monotonous tourist path. As we walked down the street, the crowd was thick with local people out and enjoying the city life. We passed many shops, bars, and vendors; who were set up right on the street with their food set up and ready to be served to the people who were walking by. This was the food I had been dying to try; it looked so much better to me than the food we had been served in the private tourist rooms of the restaurants.

After walking for a little while we finally landed on a little place with just a few people and a band that was playing reggae music in mandarin. It was just as odd as it sounded, but the band actually sounded great. They knew a few songs that we were requesting including "Country Roads" by John Denver that when played had the place erupting. Everyone in China knows that song very well.

I learned a new game that some of the locals were playing over to the side of the room. I never found out the name of the game but it involved everyone having a cup with five dice in each cup and after everyone rolls their dice on the table they keep the dice covered with their cups and you try to catch one of the other players lying about what they rolled.

Today we started with a visit to the Chinese film museum. I was unaware of the long elaborate history of Chinese film. In a sense I am still a little unaware since only a fourth of the museum had been translated into English. However I could make out that China has a very rich film background with ties to American film with highly touted actors like

Jackie Chan and Jet Lee. The Chinese film industry is also heavily censored and controlled by the government – much like everything else.

It was a little odd that the museum had little English translation because everything else around the city has a good amount of English translations like traffic signs and signs inside shops and restaurants.

After the museum we visited the Beijing Zoo and a couple of parks. At the Zoo we visited the Giant Panda exhibit. The panda's usually just eat and sleep, fortunately for us we caught them during feeding time. One park we visited had a small hill that overlooked the Forbidden City, but it was tough to fully make out the complete panorama of the view due to the thick smog. At the bottom of the hill was a beautiful park with soft green grass. I took the opportunity to kick off my shoes and rub my bear feet in it. It was soft and relaxing and felt better than any massage. However quickly after my relaxing experience I found out that it is forbidden to step on the grass because it is so fragile and there is not a lot of grass in the city so they try to protect what grass there is. The park was a peaceful escape from the city that lied right outside the park, but the choking smog invaded on the peacefulness and kept me from relaxing too much.

Tonight's supper was at the Peking Duck restaurant for the world famous Peking duck. It truly was a heap of food. We were warned not to fill up too fast because the duck was served last and that was the main reason we were there.

The duck was beautiful but to me it lacked a lot of flavor by itself. We were instructed to take small pieces of the duck, place it in a very thin tortilla looking bread, and cover it in duck sauce and slender cuts of vegetables. This gave the dish more flavor that made it delicious. The restaurant had different performers for its guest while they ate. The entire performers spoke in Chinese so at many times it was difficult to follow what was going on, but it reassembled a circus act.

At the Peking Duck I stepped away from the table to go to the restroom which turned out to be in the basement. In the basement were many other rooms including one room I found that caught my attention. The room looked like a Chinese fight club with a group of about twenty men stretching in preparation for something. There was a large wrestling map stretched across the center of the floor and a large Chinese flag draped across the far back wall.

The Forbidden City from a neighboring hill

June 30 – Day 7

This morning there is an overcast mixed in with the still thick smog. About the only way to tell there is overcast is that the streets are wet from rain. The rain has surprisingly not caused the temperature to be extremely humid, although I bet that will change as the day progresses.

Today we toured the Temple of Heaven. It was much like the other ancient architecture except it set itself apart in that it was perfectly round. The courtyard seemed a little more open and less cluttered with other buildings. To enter the Temple of Heaven one must walk down a long stone path. Before entering the pathway there is a small stone mound with a unique rock at its pinnacle. This stone is round and flat but it is easy to tell it apart from all of the other stones surrounding it. When you stand on this particular stone and speak, you can hear your own echo. No one else but the person on the stone can hear the echo.

After the temple we visited a small tea house for a tea ceremony. During the ceremony we sampled the main tea's they have here in China like the: Ginseng Oolong tea, Pu'er tea,

Litchi Black tea, Jasmine tea, Green tea and, my favorite, the fruit tea.

For lunch we were treated to a western style buffet to give us a break from the Chinese food. I hadn't realized how much I had missed mashed potatoes. Lunch was on the top floor of the Pearl Market. After we ate we were allowed to go downstairs to the market. I went back to see my friend Lulu on the third floor. She remembered me and all of the surrounding vendors seemed amused by our new friendship.

After the market we caught an acrobatics show. It was similar to the Kung Fu show but not as interesting to me. It again felt like being at a circus.

When we returned to the hotel that night, I walked down the street to the grocery store by myself. It was a great chance to explore Beijing at my own pace uninterrupted by anyone else. I took my time strolling down the street and taking in everything, from the sounds to the smells. I did the same once I found myself back in the "Wu-Mart". I studied every inch of the store. Besides the temperature inside and everything labeled in a foreign language it felt familiar. Though everything was labeled in mandarin I could recognized most things from the labels like Coke-cola and Snickers.

Temple of Heaven

July 1 – Day 8

Today is July 1st and is the 90th anniversary of the Chinese Communist party. The overcast began yesterday has really set in today. It is wet and nasty today and you cannot see a thing outside.

As we drive through the city, even after eight days I am still seeing new buildings and areas of the city I had not seen yet. The city does not seem the best suited for rain. In many places the rain water is collecting into pools in the street and sidewalks. They counter this problem with workers sweeping the water towards the drains with large brooms.

Today we began the day at the summer palace. We got a nice break from the usual tour of ancient structures with a ferry across the large lake inside the palace. Despite the thick overcast and smog, that once again limited the view, it was very peaceful.

Today we finally got to tour the Birds Nest and the Water Cube. I have been waiting almost 6 months for this particular day and my camera died before we got to the Birds Nest. I was forced to suffer at the mercies of everyone else capturing this glorious moment for me with their cameras. The Birds Nest was home of the 2008 Beijing Olympics. It was as amazing as I was expecting. It is not used as much today other than a tourist attraction. This gigantic monument to global athletic competition has now been reduced to tourists paying to drive Segways around the giant track inside the stadium.

Standing just as impressive a few hundred yards away was the Water Cube. Inside half of the cube is now a large water park. On the other half I found a large stadium looking room. As I walked through the tunnel the room opened up and there it set - the same pool that American Michael Phelps made famous by winning a gold medal in every event he swam in the 2008 Beijing Olympics. The room was spotless. There were workers on their hands and knees scrubbing off scuff marks off the floor.

The people that worked in the cube were adamant about keeping it pristine. At one point I stepped up on the railing around one of the sections of seats to snag a better view. I was quickly and sternly asked to step down and not step back up by one of the ladies working.

After a Southwestern Chinese lunch that was composed of fried fish, potatoes, and spicy chicken, we went back to old downtown Beijing. There we visited two towers. One tower was an old drum tower where we witnessed a drum show. In ancient times the drum tower was used to help the people of the city keep time.

That evening we took a rickshaw tour of a Hu Tong neighborhood. A Hu Tong is a community of lower to middle class people. They are scattered all around in Beijing. Many times you could be walking past one without even realizing it. We were fortunate enough to go into one of the homes and eat dinner with a local family. The food resembled the food we had been served in the restaurants in previous days. This made me feel a little bit better in that I felt like I had actually been eating true Chinese food the whole time and that they were not just going easy on me because I was a westerner or because some of the people in our group could not handle the sight of a cooked fish head.

The father of the house was an actual Kung Fu master. He showed us a sample of his skill which he has passed on to his three sons, one of whom is making his living teaching Kung Fu back in the US. It is no secret the father is very proud of his sons. It is easy to tell how important family is to these people. The family was very kind and generous. The mother of the home cooked so much food that despite how much I stuffed myself there was still food that was left uneaten. I tried so hard to finish what was left as to not be rude but there was just too much food.

July 2 – Day 9

It is another rainy smoggy day. We got a 5:00 am wakeup call this morning so we could catch the early train to a small town on the coast called Qinhuangdao (ch-n-hwäng-dou). While in Qinhuangdao we will visit one of Troy University's partner universities called Hebei University.

The train station in Beijing is supposedly one of, if not the largest train stations in Asia. Even at 6:00 am it is packed and seems to be running at full capacity. This train system is the main means of transportation between cities in China. The train was quiet, smooth and relaxing. The smoggy overcast almost stretched the entire way to Qinhuangdao. There were a few moments where it broke long enough to see the country side. The landscape that stretched between the two cities was endless and beautiful. The land was mostly vast flat lands of farms and small villages that were broken up every so often by mounds of rock that are or once were quarries.

Quickly after arriving in Qinhuangdao it is obviously cleaner than Beijing. Even though it is a city of about two million it is a smaller city by Chinese standards. Once we arrived we were swiftly taken to our hotel where we had to immediately get ready to meet the chancellor of Hebei. Our Hotel was the International Hotel and had a western feel inside the rooms with its woodwork on the beds, closets and doors.

After getting dressed some of us were downstairs in the lobby waiting on the rest of the group to get ready, when we were all given an instant panic attack as the sound of what seemed like gun fire rang out in the street. I was only a fraction of a second from hitting the floor behind the couch next to me before I finally realized it was only firecrackers that had been lit in the street as a part of a wedding celebration that was being held in the hotel at the same time.

When we finally made it to the university we were taken to a "meet and greet" with the administration of Hebei. Then we were taken to the dining hall on campus for a banquet. The chancellor gave us gifts from the university which was Hebei t-shirts and pins. We were joined with a few students from the university. One student in particular, Mickey, impressed me with her singing of "Country Roads" on the bus.

After lunch, and still dressed up in our semi-formal attire, we were surprised with a quick trip to a small beach. I was not going to miss anything! So I lost the bowtie and jacket, rolled up my sleeves and pants and walked out into the Bo Hai Sea. The sea directly connects to the Pacific Ocean and separates China from North Korea. The sand was a deeper tan color and felt more course than the sand back home on the coast of south Alabama and Florida. It felt great to stand in the water and lookout at the ocean and know that thousands of miles away in "that" direction, is home. It helped put in perspective how far from home I had actually made it.

After the beach it was another Olympic park and another market. In the market there was a strong combination of Chinese and Russian speaking people. Apparently this city is a Russian summer getaway spot. Steven and I found a little shop to sit down and relax as we waited for everyone else. The shop we stopped at appeared to be run by a small family whose kids – close to our age – spoke a little bit of English. Some of the guys were at another table arm wrestling so I walked over and tried my hand at it - I did not stand a chance. There English was pretty primitive. They mostly knew only basketball terms. One guy just kept asking me about Alan Iverson over and over.

Dinner, to me was a real treat. It was inside one of the luxury boxes of the local soccer stadium. This stadium was one of the soccer stadiums used in the Beijing Olympics. The venue was great! The food was the usual.

Myself, Mickey and Steven on the beach

July 3 – Day 10

After a rough night of sleep in my first night in Qinhuangdao, I was greeted with blue skies and sunshine. This is the first time I have seen blue skies since being in China.

Today we visited more sections of the Great Wall of China including the beginning of the wall which is called the Dragons Head. It stretches out over the beach and into the ocean. The beach where the Dragons Head lies is rockier than the beach from the previous day. Instead of sand bars there were large rocks protruding out of the water where people could swim out to and climb on. Out closer to the horizon in the water were dozens of large ships that were scattered about and appeared to be sitting there, waiting.

About lunch time I started feeling sick to my stomach and head and could not push on anymore. I had to take a taxi back to the hotel to rest. I really hated to miss the rest of the day's events. I do not want to miss anything.

July 4 – Day 11

Happy Independence Day from China! The smog has returned as well as piercing pain in my leg. I decided to push through the pain as not to miss anymore of the trip.

The day began with a tour of a branch of the Hebei University. I got to practice my Chinese calligraphy with the help of the local students. However during one the presentations by the students I began feeling really dizzy and had to step outside to gather myself. My friend Karli helped me outside to sit down. One of the group leaders from Hebei took us to a place where I could lay down, which turned out to be a dorm room. The school nurse came by to check on me. She gave me a z-pack and some kind of fluid to put on my leg. After some rest the group came by to pick us up and it was on to lunch. I still had not gotten my appetite back and did not eat anything.

After lunch we drove about an hour into the country to the Great Wall winery. I struggled through the whole tour. It was getting harder for me to walk on my leg. I made it all the way through the tour until I could not push through the pain anymore. Pete, who used to be an Air Force medic took a look at my leg and immediately said I needed to get to a hospital. Pete, Maple, and I took a car on the long hour and half ride back into town to the hospital. Maple is a Chinese native who had been teaching at Troy University for the past several months. She taught speaking English in China and speaking mandarin in America.

The hospital was very busy and for me confusing. It was hard for me to walk or sit on my leg but I was forced to do both as we walked back and forth between two buildings meeting with the doctor and the area to get blood samples taken. The infection is spreading from my right thigh. They think it could have been caused by some kind of bug bite.

When I got to the hospital I was running a 104 degree fever. I was lucky enough to find a bed in a private room which from what I could tell was a very unusual thing even though the private room, I think was actually a closet that had a spare bed left behind in it. There were patients practically stacked on top of each other in each room. There were even patients lined up in beds in the hallway, not waiting to be treated but actually being treated in the hallway. There were many family members there visiting with loved ones in the hospital, some had even found open beds. Many doubled up on beds to catch a quick nap.

My room was just that, a small room with a little window overlooking the street below and the side of the angled building. The only thing in the room was a small bed which sat about a foot and half off the floor, had no mattress and was as hard as wood. There was an old rolled up afghan for a pillow. Pete pointed out that the only decoration in the whole room was a small butterfly design on the end of the bed. The I.V.'s that were given to me were in glass bottles and delivered through a straight needle which I opted to have put in my arm instead of my hand, because I could not bear to be pricked in my hands. However this forced me to keep my arm straight the whole time as to not cut off the flow of the I.V. Keeping my arm straight I was unable to roll over or change positions and had to lay on my back on that bed for about six straight hours. To top everything off I got one of my favorite things of all time…the good 'ole steroid shot!

Pete and Maple went above and beyond to take care of me. Maple took care of almost everything including water and food. Pete kept me busy and distracted with stories and conversation. Five I.V.'s later my temperature got down to about 98 degrees. The hospital wanted to keep me over night, but I just wanted to go back to the hotel and then go back in the morning. After a short cab ride we made it back to the hotel about 2:00 am. I made it to my room and instantly passed out.

The Dragon's Head

July 5 – Day 12

Today was the day I was supposed to catch the train back to Beijing with the rest of my group; however Maple, Pete and I have stayed behind to spend another day at the hospital until they clear me to travel.

I at least got to sleep in for a little bit this morning, but after changing rooms because of our prolonged stay, it was back to the hospital where it was more I.V.'s and antibiotics.

My fever is only one degree higher than normal today, but the doctors still will not let me travel back to Beijing until I get the fever under control. It is looking like I will not see the rest of the group until Thursday. I am now in this small Chinese city with two people I have only known for a few months. Aside from the pain, that I have basically adjusted to by now, I am glad to be here. Much like a couple days ago when a few of our group got out and experienced the Beijing night life I feel like I am seeing the real China here.

When we got to the hospital it was about 1:00 pm and it was just as busy as the day before. There were patients still stacked in the hallway and rooms packed to capacity. There were many families there bringing meals and visiting loved ones. It was also easy to see that some families had even spent the night in the hospital so they could remain close to their loved ones. There were in some instances family members doubling up on the same single sized cot.

Today I was put in a room with other patients. It was difficult not to have an unnerving feeling from the room. The far wall of the room was dark and dirty as if it had suffered through a fire at one time. I grabbed a chair in the corner of the room by the window with another spectacular view of the side of the building; it did also have a slight view of the city too. After the nurse came in and stuck me with the day's dose of I.V. I began to do the only thing there was to do: sit, wait and watch the slow drip of my own personal mixture of antibiotics.

I watched as patients came and left. At one time there was a young 10 year-old boy who said his name was Hann who came in and sat down at the other end of the room. He appeared to be with his father, mother and older sister. He looked terrified as the nurse began to stick him with the I.V. I could not help but feel his pain. I pulled out my IPod and remembering that teachers here play "Country Roads" in the classroom to their students I began search for the closest thing to that song – once I regrettably realized it was not on my IPod. I settled on "Song of the South" by Alabama and handed my IPod to Pete to take it over to the boy. He put in the headphones and Pete pressed play. The boy had a puzzled look on his face through the whole song. His mother began chuckling at him and turned to smile at me as if to thank me in some way. Even if he did not like it at least it distracted him for a short time. After the song was over he handed the IPod back to Pete who brought it back to me. The boy then took out his cell phone and began playing his own music. It was a wide variety of Chinese songs. The first song sounded like a national anthem-march type of song. The second sounded like a Chinese version of Alvin and the Chipmunks. After about an hour Hann finally got to leave. He and his family all waved and said:

Good Bye - 再见 (Zàijiàn) –"Zye-Chen"

After Hann and his family left it was then only Pete, Maple and me left in the room. We killed the rest of our time with conversations that turned into deep ideological discussions and Pete's inescapable humor. Pete and I had a little fun whenever a nurse would come in to change my I.V.'s we would try out our best pick-up lines on the nurse. Of course the nurses not knowing any English did not respond at all to our one liner's.

My I.V.'s finished about 7:00 pm and we were able to leave the hospital. The doctor had me on a particular diet that included no pork and fresh vegetables. Weary of Chinese food, Pete and I were able to talk Maple into letting us grab some KFC. Unfortunately it was not the same KFC as back home. There were no green beans, coleslaw or even biscuits. The mash potatoes and gravy lacked hardly any flavor and there was no salt or pepper to help with the lack of flavor. However it was still enough of a break from the regular Chinese food to offer a small dose of relief.

July 6 – Day 13

This trip has quickly turned into the opposite of what I had hoped it would be. Despite the pain and discomfort though, I feel like I am receiving my own one of a kind experience. Being my third day in a row to go back to the hospital I have seen enough of the hospital. I am ready to be back in Beijing with the rest of the group and my friends to experience more of the country.

One thing in particular that has really begun to wear on me is how everyone at the hospital stares at me. It is aggravating how despite when I look back at them to acknowledge that I know they are starring they continue to glare at me with blank mysterious expressions. I realize they are not trying to be rude but its difficult not to walk away with that impression.

In the hospital today I was put me in what appeared to be a newer and cleaner section of the hospital. There was more good news; only three I.V.'s today! Pete and I celebrated when we heard this news. I know this whole hospital trip is wearing on me, but I cannot imagine how bored and aggravated this must be to Pete and Maple. They are doing a good job of hiding it though, and it is keeping me in good spirit.

The room they put me in was much bigger with many rows of reclining chairs, each with its own I.V. hook on a pole that extended up the side of the chair. One thing about this room though, was each row of chairs faced each other and instead of a window view I had to try not to make too much awkward eye contact with the people across the aisle.

As I am away from the group who is now in Beijing and on their regular schedule, I realize I am going to miss the last trip to the Pearl Market and my last chance to buy gifts for everyone back home. So after talking Maple into breaking my rice and fresh vegetable diet again and visit McDonald's for lunch, I also convinced her into allowing me to visit a local market here in Qinhuangdao.

The market here was a little different. Vendors were less aggressive and prices were harder to haggle. I needed another luggage bag for the trip home and I was only able to talk the vendor down from ¥120 to ¥90 – not as spectacular as my previous encounters. Maple laughs at my haggling skills and how much I seem to enjoy it.

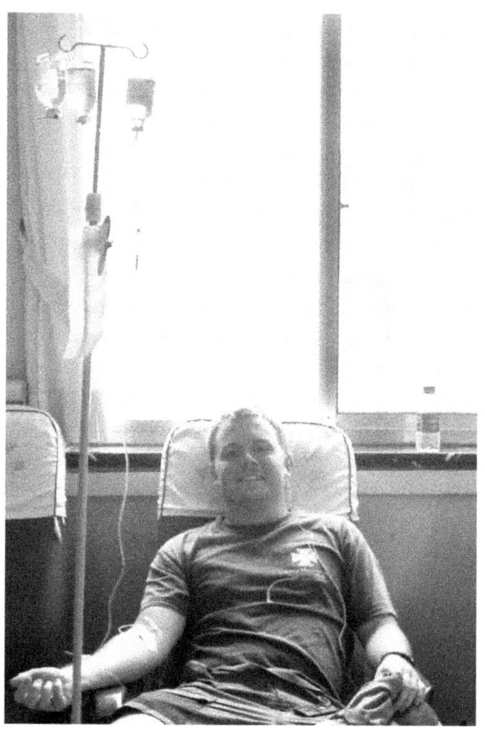

July 7 – Day 14

Yesterday was an overall short day as I am sure today will be too. I am feeling worn down and, as much as I do not want to admit it, I am about ready to go home. I have had just about enough of the constant discomfort and poking and prodding by people who I cannot understand what they are saying. If I was feeling any better I would want to stay longer, but I have been away from the group now for too long and I am losing my optimism.

To make matters worse I recently acquired a bad case of the hick-ups which constantly come and go. I kept getting them in the middle of the night making it hard to sleep. As it turns out this could be attributed to the medicine they have been giving me.

Today it was back to the hospital, to the same room and same chair as the day before. After three quick rounds of I.V.'s I was finally good to go!

As I was lying in my room before we left for the hospital this morning the Chancellor of Hebei University and some members of his administration stopped by the hotel to check on me. They brought flowers and were very friendly. Despite the language barrier we joked and cut up just like we were all friends. I could not thank them enough for their hospitality.

I talked Maple into KFC for lunch again. I have found it is pretty easy to veer her off of my suggested medical diet. Her sister joined us and even brought me bananas which helped with the hick ups.

After lunch and a quick nap back at the hotel it was on to the train station for our 5:30 pm train. We're FINALLY headed back to Beijing.

Knowing that tomorrow I will be getting on the plane to head back home I felt myself getting a little nostalgic in the car to the train station. Despite the events I have suffered through in this little Chinese town, I tried to take it all in one last time. I took a good hard look at the city, its people and the coast one more time knowing that this could be the last time I might ever see any of these things. The same feeling hit me on the train to Beijing as well as the chaotic van ride back to the hotel. Driving through the city one last time I was looking at a city that now made more sense and seemed more conventional to me now than it had two weeks ago. I have experienced a culture that has been going on about its business this whole time only thousands of miles away from where I have lived my whole life. I feel like I have learned a lot about Chinese culture and what it has brought these people. Good or bad, who is to say, it has made these people who they are and I am truly thankful for the chance to peek in and catch a glimpse of it.

Epilogue

After the long flight back to Chicago and what seemed like an even longer flight from Chicago to Atlanta, I finally made it back to home in north Alabama. Though it felt much better being back, I was still not out of the woods.

I had to check into Huntsville Hospital the day after I arrived home. The doctors at the hospital in China mostly worked to get my fever down to the point where I could travel. They however did little to stop the infection in my leg. This led to me spending four more days in an American hospital.

In the end I had to have surgery and spent close to a month on home bed rest after being released from the hospital. It was unclear as to the exact cause of the infection, but by the end I had a laundry list of ailments to overcome.

The trip, needless to say, turned into much more than I had prepared for, but I would not have traded a minute of it. It was a once in a lifetime kind of trip. The infection I had picked up, though inconvenient opened a window into a part of China not many get even close to seeing. The time I spent in the hospital allowed me to cross paths with people who have been living out their lives thousands of miles away.

It also allowed me to make new friends. I do not think I could ever thank Pete and Maple enough for everything they had done for me; though I have told them many times. For me the trip began as a part of an anthropology study and I gained more firsthand experience about the Chinese culture than I ever could on the tourist route.

The prayers of my family and friends are ultimately what got me home, and I am forever thankful for every pray and every person. I am especially thankful to my parents who got me through my days at the hospital here at home, and who had to sweat it out while I was in a hospital thousands of miles away.

It took some time to recover from this trip but I am excited and ready for the next journey.

Thank You

I would like to thank you for reading my story. If you would like to see more pictures and videos from the trip you can find them at:

BtheMaxChinaStudy.tumblr.com

I am also glad to receive any questions or comments on my work. You can find more "View from My Chair" trips and even contact me through my blog:

ViewFromMyChair.tumblr.com

Thank You,

Benjamin Maxwell

www.ingramcontent.com/pod-product-compliance
Ingram Content Group UK Ltd.
Pitfield, Milton Keynes, MK11 3LW, UK
UKHW020217250726
13967UKWH00001B/52

9 781300 314196